IDYLLS

HYMNS

DIRGES

CHARLES PERDU

ISBN: 0-7596-6644-X

This book is printed on acid free paper.

1stBooks - rev. 01/19/02

TABLE OF CONTENTS

LOVE LOST AND FOUND

A BENIGN BESTIARY

ATROCITIES OF PEACE

INCIDENTALS

LOVE LOST AND FOUND

SEARCHING FOR ADRIANA

HYMN TO THE EPIC MUSE

MOST FAIR CALLIOPE, WHERE MAY I FIND
A MAID OF FLESH GRACED WITH THY NOBLE MIND
SET IN A FORM FULL FAIR AS THINE TO SEE,
ONE YET POSSESSED OF UNIQUE CONSTANCY
TO EPIC DREAM AND PRINCIPAL IN FACE
OF MULTITUDES INSIPID AND DEBASED
WITH VANITY, FRIVOLITY AND WHIM?
WHERE MAY I CHANCE UPON A MAIDEN SLIM
AND LITHE WITH VIRTUE'S FLEXIBILITY,
WHOSE GUILELESS EYE CAN VEIL NO TREACHERY,
BUT MUST REFLECT
EACH HONEST AND PURE THOUGHT
EXPRESSED BY LIPS
BOTH VIRGIN AND LOVE FRAUGHT,
WHO HAVING ONCE DECLARED HER NOBLE MIND
WILL NOT RETRACT IT, BUT INCREASE IN KIND
HER WHOLESOME LOVE AND FAVORS UNTO ME
WHICH I'LL RETURN WITH RASH IDOLATRY?
IF SUCH A ONE EXISTS, HEROINE MUSE,
HER PRESENCE MY WHOLE WORLD
WOULD SOON TRANSFUSE
INTO A VAST ARENA OF DELIGHT
NO EVIL OR DISTORTED THING COULD BLIGHT,
ALL OBJECTS PURIFIED IN ADORATION
OF HER CHASTE INTELLECT'S INTERPRETATION.

INVITATION

SUN SHINES
SULLEN FIELDS SPRING GREEN
FUZZY BUDS GLEAM ON EVERY BRANCH.
HEAT SEEPS THROUGH
BURSTS OF SPORTIVE GUSTS
SWIRLING FRESH TIDINGS OF HIGH PRESSURE HOPE
ACROSS A SULKING WORLD.

RATTLING SHUTTERS PRIMLY PRATTLE THE NEWS.

WHAT THEN SHALL WE DO?
WRAP OUR LONGINGS TIGHT
IN FRIGHT AND COLD DESPAIR,
OR FLING OFF SHROUDS
TO VANISH AS THE CLOUDS
CAREENING
DANCE BENEATH A PREENING SKY?

PROCLAIM BRIGHT FAITH
SANCTIFY THIS OMNIPRESENT URGE.
LOVE
AND LOVING MERGE
WITH UNARTICULATED STIRRING OF EACH DEEP
INEFFABLE FORCE THAT SEEDS, SEEDS, SEEDS

BREED IN PLEASURED GAZE OF THE INFINITE I.

PROPOSAL FOR AN EDIFICE

WHAT ARE WE TWO? VIRTUALLY LITTER?
TWO BILLIONTHS OF A SPAWN OF SENTIENT DROSS
SEAFLUNG, FOGGED, AWASH,
FROTH ON THE LUNATIC TIDE
OF A FATHOMLESS GULF?
ENOUGH OF DRIFT AND DOUBT.
SEIZE RANDOM NATURE'S SUBSTANCE
IN YOUR HANDS
AND CAST WITH ME UPON HOPE'S NARROW SHORE
A VALIANT PILE OF LOVE'S PERSISTING GRIT.
IN MOULDING LET OUR BODIES FORM GOD'S PLAN
TO THWART THE RHYTHMED LAVE
OF PURBLIND TIME.
WE'LL RAISE ON ADORATION'S RAWGRAINED KEEP
DEEP JOY'S ENDURING ENSIGN
TO FLOAT UNFURLED AND UNDEFILED
FROM AGE TO AGE
DESPITE THE ACRID BITE OF FINITY'S GALES,
A SHEER, SUBLIME, ENTOWERED TESTAMENT
OF OUR LITTORAL VIRTUE.

SUPPLICATION

ACCEPT THESE ADDLED CHARDS
OF ASPIRATION
NOT CRITICALLY,
WITH REASON'S CHILL, CURT SCOWL,
BUT GENTLY, AS A GODDESS
KNEELS TO BATHE
HER SIMPLE, FERVID, FUMBLING VOTARY
IN TENDER DROPS
OF PITY'S PASSIONED GRACE.

CONSIDER NOT THE ERRORS OF MY SCROLL.
THEIR TOLL'S TOO LONG TO TELL.
THINK, RATHER, OF A PRISONER GRIMLY MOLING
WITH TOOLS SCARCE FIT FOR USE
THROUGH TIERS OF HOLLOW TASKS
PILED YEAR ON YEAR,
BLINDLY COMPASSED IN A BRISTLING PIT
BY HOPE'S ELUSIVE FLICKER.

SCAN LIGHTLY ALL MY FLAWS.
YOUR ARTLESS CHARM
CAN TURN AMORPHOUS CLAY
TO BRILLIANT, BURNISHED FORM,
AND TWINE ENTANGLED SHOOTS OF MUDDLED ZEAL
ALONG LOVE'S INFINITE THREAD OF DEDICATION.

HEED AT LAST MY PLEA
FOR PATIENT TESTING.
IS HEAVEN HOPE'S ILLUSION,
HELL LIFE'S FACT?
CAN NATURE NOURISH EVERY FAVOR
                IN ONE PERFECT MOULD
YET LET COMPASSION LANGUISH UNCONJOINED?
HAS TRUST TOO FINE A GRAIN FOR USE AGAIN?
SAY, RATHER, WATER'S DRY,
GLUM EARTH IS VAPOR,
AND MYSTIC MULTITUDES OF SQUIRMING SEED
ARE LIFELESS, COCKLED LITTER, MOCK AND SHAM.

FOR ELSE, I BLOOM TO NO PURPOSE

COME BE MY LOVE, AND LIVE IN A DREAM WITH ME,
LIP TO LIP, TREMULOUSLY,
AS THE VIVID, SILKEN, AIRY BUTTERFLY
IS WAFTED, FLUTTERS,
AND FALLS TO FRAGILE DELIGHT
UPON A CUP OF NECTAR.

AS A SCRUBBY WEED
FULLBLOWN BY NATURE'S SUBTLE ALCHEMY
MAY THRALL THE BRILLIANT CREATURE,
LULLING IT WITH SUCCULENCE
IN THE BUZZY, HUSHED HEAT
OF A SUMMER MEADOW,
TO LOLL INDEFINITE, ENFOLDED, CAPTURED,
THUS DO I HOPE TO HOLD YOU CONSTANT TO ME,
FORGETFUL OF A HOST OF DAZZLING HONEYS,
LOST ON A WISP OF BLISS,
STUNNED IN THE SPLENDOR OF RAPTURE.

WE'LL PASS THIS VAST, BRIEF, SOPORIFIC SEASON
FREELY LOCKED,
IN SWEETNESS LAY OUR REASON,
LET THE DRONE GO ON, UNHEEDED.

PETALS WILL FALL,
KEEN HUES MUST LOSE THEIR LUSTRE.
LET US SO CLING
IN DELICATE ENCHANTMENT,
COCOONING AGAINST WINTER,
THAT WHEN THAT GREAT, GROSS, HAIRY BEAST CALLED DEATH
STALKS FROM A SODDEN FOREST
TO CRUSH WITH CLOVEN HOOF
DRAB, BRITTLE REMNANTS OF A SUNNY PAST
THE BLOW WILL FIND US STILL IN LOVE ENCLASPED.

OR, IF SOMEHOW OUR PARADISE BE MISSED
BY AWED, BRUTISH NATURE,
THEN LET US SEED FRESH SPRING'S FRENETIC JOY
LOVING THE ORBIT ROUND,
BOUND IN SILK SECURITY,
WARM, GREEN, BURGEONING,
TREMBLING ON A KISS.

FIRST LOVE

I DREAMED OF PERFECTION
FAIR VISIONS I KNEW
I SEARCHED IN DEJECTION
AT LAST I FOUND YOU.

AS GAUNT EXPLORERS ROUND A CAMPFIRE SCANNED
RUDE MAKESHIFT MAPS OF AN UNCHARTED LAND
AND THEN PLUNGED ON INTO THE DISTANT, DIM
DOMAINS THAT LAY BEYOND THE SETTLED RIM,
SUBDUING ELEMENTS, PAIN, DOUBT AND FEAR,
UNTIL AT LAST WITH HOLLOW, FRENZIED CHEER
THEY BURST UPON A VISTA VAST AND NEW,
THUS DID I FEEL WHEN FIRST I LOOKED ON YOU.

YOUR LOVELINESS CHARMED ME,
RESIST HOW I MIGHT,
COMPLETELY DISARMED ME,
I LOVED YOU AT SIGHT.

THE AWE AND WONDER RUDE CAVE DWELLERS FELT
AS IN A MYSTIC CIRCLE FIRST THEY KNELT
AROUND A FLICKRING FIRE NEWLY FOUND,
SEED OF A LIGHTNING SHAFT
THAT STABBED TO GROUND,
AND BLINDLY WORSHIPPING ITS HEAT AND LIGHT
DREAMED VAGUELY
HOW THEIR NEW GOD-WEAPON MIGHT
REVEAL TO THEM A WORLD

WARM, BRIGHT AND NEW,
THAT PRIMAL REVERENCE I FELT FOR YOU.

ONE IDYLLIC SEASON
WE LAUGHED AND WERE GAY,
UNTIL FRIGID REASON
DROVE LOVE'S WARMTH AWAY.

AS NATURE GAMBOLS IN THE GLOW OF JUNE
INTENSELY, KNOWING THAT SEPTEMBER SOON
WILL FROWN UPON FAIR SUMMER'S CAREFREE WAYS,
THUS DID WE TWO CRAM SUN-ENCHANTED DAYS
AND BALMY, BLISSFUL, STAR-ENCRUSTED NIGHTS
PROFUSELY WITH LOVE'S INNOCENT DELIGHTS.
BUT SMILING SUMMER LEFT ME DEEP IN GLOOM
AS AUTUMN'S AWFUL ADVENT
TOLLED LOVE'S DOOM.

FOR OTHER DREAMS BOUND YOU,
AND PLANS LONG SINCE MADE
DESCENDED AROUND YOU.
I LOOKED ON, DISMAYED.

IF DYING OF A DREADFUL MALADY,
A WEARY CHEMIST SEEKING REMEDY
CONCOCTED IN HIS VIALS AT LAST A CURE,
A POTION RENDERING RECOVERY SURE,
THEN FOUND HIS ILLNESS SPREAD TO SUCH DEGREE
THAT SCHEMING DEATH MUST CLAIM HER VICTORY,
NO GREATER SADNESS COULD HE KNOW THAN I,
AS FATE DECREES THAT WE MUST SAY GOODBYE.

ENRAPT

UPON AWAKING IN THE NUPTIAL BED
WE CLOVE UNTO EACH OTHER'S EYES, AND READ
ALL MYSTIC, MUTE, INEFFABLE
SOARING THOUGHT
WHICH MAN HAS VAGUELY DREAMED
AND VAINLY SOUGHT
SINCE ADAM WONDERED
WHY AND WHAT AND WHERE.

TRUE BELIEVERS

THERE ARE NO ATHEISTS IN LOVE.
A FOCUSSED PEACE BELOW, ABOVE
OBSCURES TRAVAILS OF EVIL,
THE UNIVERSE MADE GOOD
LIP ENGULPED IN LIP
HIP EMBRACING HIP
DELIRIUM OF UNITY
TRANSCENDENT GOD MADE RAPTURE.

FOR ERI

FRAGILE MAIDEN, TOSSED IN THRONGS
YOUR TINKLING DREAMS RANG OUT ABOVE THE DIN
TO WAKE MY DEADENED HEART,
LONG PINNED BY THONGS
OF SINUOUS DESPAIR THAT RENT ME DIM.
CAN LOVE SPRING FORTH AFRESH
AND PRUDENCE FALL
TRICKED BY MEMORY BUBBLES PRICKED ON TIME?
HERE NOW, AND NOW, AND NOW, TWO ONE IN ALL
TOMORROW COMES, PAST, PRESENT MERGE SUBLIME.
LET BRAZEN MINDS THEIR PALTRY BALANCE WEIGH.
LET BRAID ENCRUSTED BRAINS
WAN WAR GAMES PLAY.
LOVE'S WIT UPSETS FALSE WEIGHTS
THAT MEN DEMEAN,
ARRAYS VAST WAYS TO VALUE PEARLS UNSEEN.
CHEATS, CAST OFF YOUR SCALES!
DEMEAN NO MORE WITH MALICE
MY CUT RUBIED HEART,
OR ERI'S PRICELESS CHALICE.

LAMENT

SHE'S GONE,
LIKE A DREAM THAT SLIPPED AWAY.
SHE'S GONE,
THERE IS LITTLE MORE TO SAY.
NOW MATTER HOW I YEARN
SHE NEVER WILL RETURN.
SHE'S GONE.

I MOURN.
LIFE IS GAUNT WHEN LOVE IS GONE.
I MOURN.
LIKE A DISMAL, SUNLESS DAWN.
THIS LONELINESS I FEEL
STILL SEEMS, SOMEHOW, UNREAL.
I MOURN.

NAMELESS THINGS

THE SUN CAME OUT AT LAST
SOFTLY MELTING A PALL OF CLOUDS
STILL BROODING IN THE SKY,
BLUNTING THE RAW EDGE OF WINTER IN THE AIR.

GREY WATER GLISTENED
DESPITE ITS SOMBER HUE,
LAUGHING BACK AT THE GLAD NEWS
BEFORE IT HAD BEEN FULLY HEARD,
AND LAZY SUNDAY PEOPLE
LIFTED THEIR EYES, SMILING
TO SEE THE DAZZLING RAYS PROBE THROUGH.

THE CITY SIGHED
TENDERLY.

WHAT WAS IT THAT YOU GAVE TO ME
FROM CUPPED HANDS
                    AND OUTSTRETCHED FINGERS,
BLOWN GENTLY
WITH LIPS OF SWEET, SOFT WARMTH
AND EYES THAT SCREAMED OF JOY
WITH SUCH A SILENCE OF INTENSITY?

NAMELESS THINGS II

THE NIGHT WE LAY SO CLOSE
THAT I COULD SEE OF YOU
IN THE GLOW OF THE CANDLE FLAME
ONLY A DAZZLING REFLECTION,
AS OF SUN
BOUNDING OFF WATER IN MY EYES,
YOU CRIED.

AND THOUGH I KISSED AWAY EACH TEAR
AS BEST I MIGHT,
I KNEW THOSE VERY KISSES, LENT NOT PLEDGED,
WERE CANKERS IN YOUR HEART,
THE GNARL OF PAIN.

NOW THAT YOU ARE RESIGNED
TO THE TERMS WHICH WE LAY DOWN WITH,
AND READY TO DISMISS ALL BUT A MEMORY,
I, TOO, GROW NUMB
STUDYING YOUR EYES...

YOUR EYES.
OH, GOD,
        THAT LOVELINESS COULD EVER BE SO REAL,
AND FEEL THE CHOKING GORGE OF TEARS
        RISE IN ME, TOO.

IT IS YOUR TURN
TO WISTFULLY SMILE BACK,
AND PLUNGE THE BRUTAL CARELESSNESS I FORGED
DEEP,
TWISTING,

INTO THE HEART OF ME.

WERE YOU LESS KIND, LESS GENTLE,
LESS SUBLIME,
I MIGHT MUSE POMPOUSLY
ON THE SPECIOUS JUSTICE OF YOUR PLACID SCORN,
AND CHEW THE BLOATING CUD OF GUILT FORESWORN.
YET I KNOW
THAT YOU ARE BUT RESIGNED
QUIETLY, DULY, UTTERLY
AND THAT I, TOO, MUST NOW BE CONTENT
TO SINK BACK TO THE SHALLOW SLOUGH
OF UNCOMMITED MEDIOCRITY
WHICH I MYSELF DID DREDGE
LONG, LONG AGO,
TO FLOAT WITH LANGUID SLOTH
IN THAT DANK DITCH,
THINKING EVER,
ALL MY DAYS
OF THE SIGHT I CAUGHT OF THE SEA,
OF THE FATHOMLESS SEA...

IN THE CHILL BURN OF MOURNING

OTHER IDYLLS HAVE I KNOWN
OTHER ARMS TO CALL MY OWN
OTHER HEARTACHES HAVE I SOWN
STILL YOUR LOVE RETURNS.

STALKING ME THROUGH SILENT YEARS
STIFLING JOY WITH STILLBORN TEARS
LOVE I QUENCHED STILL FLAMES AND SEARS
LOVE FOR YOU STILL BURNS.

FLIPPANTLY I LAUGHED GOODBYE
SMILING, CHIDED DOWNCAST EYE
KISSED AWAY EACH SWEET, SAD SIGH
NOW MY HEART, TOO, YEARNS.

HAUNTING, TAUNTING, MOCKING ME
DRIVING TO ACTIVITY
A MIND IMPALED ON MEMORY
BARBED SPIT THAT DULL TIME TURNS.

TAINTED DREAMS OF WHAT MIGHT BE
PROMPT THIS FUTILE THRENODY
BARREN YEARS REMAIN TO ME
THE WAGE INDIFFERENCE EARNS.

LOVE CREEPS BACK

LOVE CREEPS BACK LIKE A LITTLE WAG DOG
TO NUZZLE THE PALM THAT CUFFED IT,
TO PUZZLE CALLOUSED FINGERTIPS
WITH SOFT, PERSISTING KISSES.

WHAT CAN ONE DO WITH THIS GROVELING MUTE?
KICK IT AWAY?
IGNORE IT?
TURN IT OUT IN THE WORLD AGAIN
HOPING THE COLD WILL KILL IT?

SOONER ONE'S HEART WILL WITHER AND CRACK,
SOONER ONE'S BRAIN WILL PLUMMET
DOWN TO THE BOWELS TO REVEL AND ROT,
SOONER ONE'S SHOES WILL STAND EMPTY.

REACTION TO THE NEWS

SO LONG AS YOU WERE THERE
I FELT, SOMEHOW, SECURE,
WANDERING, BLUNDERING
FAR FROM HOME.
NOW VIOLENCE
WHICH WAS NO PART OF YOU
HAS PLACED A CLAIM
TO BANISH YOU TO HIS DEMONIC WORLD.

THE REASON I DO NOT YET FEEL YOUR LOSS
MAY BE
THAT THE ESSENCE OF YOU
WHICH IS WHAT YOU GAVE
REMAINS
BEYOND THE PETTY PUTS AND CALLS OF LIVING,
BONE DEEP
INDESTRUCTIBLE,
AS IT HAS BEEN,
UNFORGETTABLE, UNQUENCHABLE, UNDIMINISHED
THESE LONG YEARS.

WHEN I SPOKE TO MY CONSCIENCE
IT WAS TO YOU.
IT IS TO YOU,
THE PERFECT MIRROR OF MY ILL-PERCEIVED SELF,
THAT I MUST ALWAYS TURN
TO SEEK THE REAL.

HOW CAN I FEEL A LOSS?
YOUR GENTLE SMILE,
YOUR UTTER UNDERSTANDING
WARM ME STILL,

TODAY
AND WILL TOMORROW,
AS THEY EVER HAVE THROUGH MINDLESS TIME.

I, WHO PAINED YOU SORELY,
REJOICE
THAT YOU HAVE PASSED BEYOND THE LIP OF PAIN,
PAST FORCED CONCILIATION
TO ALL THE GLOSSED IGNOBLENESS OF LIFE,
WHOLLY YOUR ESSENTIAL SELF AT LAST,
UNASSAILABLE
INDIVISIBLE PERFECTION.

YOU REMAIN
A MODEL TO LIVE BY
A VISION TO STRIVE FOR.

DAWN BURIAL

A NEW DAY!
AND HERE, ETERNAL NIGHT.
TO THINK I'LL WITNESS TWENTY THOUSAND DAWNS,
AND LIE ALONE
                    THROUGH TWENTY THOUSAND NIGHTS,
LOST
IN A DESERT OF BLACKNESS
WHILE LIFE TWITTERS AROUND ME.

WHY SHOULD I LIVE,
A STERILE INTERLOPER
WEDGED BETWEEN CONSCIENCE AND DEATH,
GRASPING BLOODY RELICS,
RASPING MY REASON TO SHREDS
ON BARBED REGRET,
THIS BARREN BODY SUCKING VAPID BREATH
TO FAN A FLAME THAT SEARS A LIVID BRAIN?
MY GUTS CRY OUT FOR DEATH
TO STOP THIS THROBBING.

BUT IF IT CEASED
AND I COULD BE NO MORE,
DRIFT IN ETHER,
THEN, PERHAPS, I COULD NOT THINK OF YOU,
NEVER FEEL THESE LIPS
                    PRESSED SPEAKING INTO MINE,

OR KNOW THESE FINGERS, TENDERLY CARESSING.
TO FOUNDER FOREVER IN A VOID DEVOID OF YOU,
OF THOSE IMPASSIONED EYES...

NEVER AGAIN, NOT EVEN IN A DREAM,
TO PLUNGE INTO THE SOFT, WARM,
TREMULOUS NIMBUS OF HEAVEN...
NEVER TO KNOW THE UNPLUMBED ECSTACY
OF PENETRATING THESE SWEET LOVE FLUNG THIGHS,
OF MERGING FLESH AND SOUL
WITH LIMBS AND EYES,
IT'S A DESTINY I SWEAR I CAN'T ENDURE.

NOW MANHOOD'S ONLY TORMENT, NOT A FLOWER,
A PISTILLESS STAMEN,
AN OVERLOADED FILAMENT
BURNING INCANDESCENT
IN SUBSTANCE SEEKING SHADOW.
I'LL TUCK YOU IN WITHOUT THE BANAL RITES,
AND CURSE AT GOD FOR MAKING BEAUTY MORTAL.

IF I COULD BURY REASON IN THIS SOD
I'D CHANT SOME SOMBER LITANY
TO DROWN THE CARELESS CHIRPING OF THE BIRDS,
AND SEND YOU DIRGING
TO A GRACIOUS PARADISE.

HOW CAN MEN MOCK AT DEATH
WITH HYPOCRITIC MOUTHING?

THE GAPING CAVERN GULPS YOU IN BLACK SILENCE
AND ECHOES BACK ALL PIOUS LAMENTATION
AS IDIOTIC GURGLING.
IT'S BLANK,
NOTHING,
THE END OF A SENSELESS BEATING.

BUT BY OUR LOVE,
I'LL USE THIS LONELY PISTON
WHILE IT LASTS
TO THUMP FOR DREAMS WE FASHIONED
IN THE PAST,
AND LACE OUR HEAVEN
CLOSER TO GOD'S EARTH.

EPITAPH II

RATIONAL SURVIVAL IN THIS WORLD ENTAILS
BLUNTING OF QUICK CHARITY AND GRACE
SENSIBLE RESOLUTION NOT TO FEEL
TOO KEENLY
        WONDERS WHICH THE HEART PERCEIVES
ECSTACIES OF SOARING ASPIRATION
THE TRAGIC BREAKING LOSS OF HOPES BENUMBED
BY PRUDENT PASSIONS, CALCULATING LOVES,
WEEKDAY ACTS OF SUNDAY MORNING CHRISTIANS.
BRIGHT, BOUYANT BOUNDLESS YEARNING
                BY GLAD HEARTS
IS INCOMPATIBLE WITH CUNNING SCHEMES.
INTENSITY UPSETS THE MEASURED PACE
OF PROGRESS TOWARD THE BEST DULL MEN CAN SEE.

HERE LIES THE END OF ONE UNSULLIED DREAM
TOO BEAUTIFUL, TOO BRIGHT, TOO FRESH, TOO KEEN
TO STAY THIS EARTH, AND PURE DELIGHT DEMEAN.

EPITAPH III

O, LARK, WHO STROVE TO FLY WITH FLAWS INBORN,
THAT KEPT YOU EARTHBOUND, SINGING TO THE SKY,
O, RARE INTENSE CAPACITY FOR JOY
THAT COULD NOT BEAR THE PAIN OF LIFE FORLORN,
YOUR FITFULL, FRIGHTENED STRUGGLES TO ENDURE
VEILED BALEFUL FRAILTIES DEFYING CURE
REVEALED A NATURE TENDER, FRAGILE, PURE,
NOW FREE AT LAST FROM DUST OF FUTILE STRIVING.
O, TREASURE LOST, TO GRACE GROSS LIFE NO MORE.

LORD, HAVE MERCY ON US,
WHO COULD NOT HELP HER PAIN.
IN HER GENTLE WAY GIVE ABSOLUTION
FROM STARK, UNBLINKING TRUTH
THROUGH STRICKEN YEARS.
CREATE HER HEAVEN TO CONSOLE THE LIVING,
THAT SHE MAY SOAR AND SING DELIGHTED THERE.

A BENIGN BESTIARY

CHIRP

BIRDS IN PUDDLES BATHE
CHIC, FLUTTERING FROLIC
HOPPING, NODDING, SPATTERING SPLASH
FLUFFCLUSTERS OF FEATHERS
BUCOLIC.

IN THE PATIENT POOL

THE PUFFTHROAT FROG
BLINKS
SQUAT AND BLOATED
HUNCHING IN THE POND
HIDING BY THE POD
WAITING FOR A PRINCESS.
IS THERE A KINDLY GOD?

TRAJECTORY

DUCKS FLASH BY
GREEN-WHITE-BROWN
EARTHTONES IN FLIGHT
PROJECTING EAGER NECKBEAKS
FRANTIC BEATING OF LIFE
TOWARD AN INFINITE BLUE.

LURK

HINGED, HAIRLINE LEGS
BLACK BULBOUS CRAVING POUCH
ON GOSSAMER SYMMETRY.
MAGNIFIED MANDIBLES
STILL
MENACE PATIENTLY.
STICKY DEATH AWAITS UNWARY PREY.
EVERYTHING MUST EAT AS BEST IT MAY.

CROCODILE

HERE LIE I
ENSCALED AGAINST A HOSTILE WORLD.
BUTTERFLIES IGNORE ME
ALAS
I WOULD BEFRIEND THEM.
IS FEAR BY OTHERS
SUFFICIENT COMPENSATION
FOR WATERLOGGED SERENITY?

PRAGMATICAT

CONSIDER THE CAT:
IT NAPS AND GROWS FAT,
BUT KEEPS IN TONE BY STEALTH AND STRIKE
GAINST MOUSES, LIZARDS, AND THE LIKE.
THE CAT FRETS NOT FOR GOD OR MAN,
ITS PURRS AND SHRIEKS SAY JUST "I AM."

THE TWO OF US

A ROBIN WATCH THE SUN GO DOWN?
“RIDICULOUS!” YOU SAY.
AND I CONCEDE YOU’RE DOUBTLESS RIGHT,
BUT JUST THE OTHER DAY...

HE PERCHED ATHWART MY WINDOW BOX,
A QUIZZICAL FLUFF OF A BIRD.
HE BLINKED HIS EYE, AND COCKED HIS HEAD,
INTENT ON SOME WORM SQUIRM HE’D HEARD.
AND AS HE PAUSED THERE, HARKING,
THE RED SUN CAUGHT HIS EYE.
FORGOTTEN WAS HIS DINNER,
HIS MATE, HIS WILL TO FLY,
HE TILTED HIS BEAK TOWARD THE SUNSET
ECSTATICALLY, EVEN AS I.

TOGETHER, NOT RUFFLING A MUSCLE,
THE TWO OF US WATCHED THE DAY PASS,
THE ROBIN PERCHED ON THE WINDOW BOX,
THE OTHER BIRD BACK OF THE GLASS.

ATROCITIES OF PEACE

POVERTY'S CHILD

BRED FROM LUST
GESTATED IN NEGLECT
WOMBSTIFLED
NURSERIED IN WASTE
PUBERTIED IN WANT'S BRUTALITIES
UNKEMPT, UNSKILLED, CRIPPLED BY DESPAIR,
LIGHT OF HOPE SNUFFED OUT IN WANTON RIOT...
BEWARE THIS TORTURED CHILD, AMERICA,
THE PRICE YOU BOTH WILL PAY.

CRACK BABY

CHICKEN BONES UNDER PARCHMENT SKIN
STARING EYES TOO BIG, TOO BRIGHT
REFLECTING HORRORS FELT NOT SEEN,
BLIND NEED,
THE ADDICTED TWITCH
THE DESPERATE CONTINUUM
                    OF STRETCH AND REACH
FOR INSENSATE OBLIVION.
MOTHER, WHAT HAVE YOU DONE?

ROMP

SPRING FRAGRANCE
ENGULFS THE VIRGIN SENSES
OF CHILDREN
ROLLICKING CLOSE TO THE EARTH
LOLLING IN DUSTY MEADOWS
ROLLING IN STALKS OF WEEDGRASS
WADING IN THE CREEKBED
SPLASHING RAINBOW PUDDLES.
HOW ARE THEY TO APPREHEND
THE FORMULATED MENACES
OF CALCULATING STRANGERS
DUMPING UNSEEN POISONS
INTO EARTH AND WATER
INTO BEGUILING SKIES
TASTELESS
GUILTLESS
PROFITABLE MEN
KILLING NATURE'S BOUNTY
MAIMING UNBORN CHILDREN
DISCLAIMING SHORTENED LIVES
DISTORTED FAMILIES
DECADES OF REMEDIES
UNAFFORDABLE
UNREPORTABLE
IN DEDUCTIBLE BOARDROOMS.

BARRIO

MEXICO CITY

WHERE ARE THE ANCIENT STALWART WARRIORS?
WHERE ARE THE STOIC SONS OF TLALPAN
BUILDERS OUT OF DOVETAILED GRANITE
OF GREAT TEMPLES, STILL STRONG STANDING?

PROUD WITH A STRENGTH
THAT CONQUERED NATURE,
HEWERS OF STONE THAT PLOTTED PLANETS,
AUTHORS OF A RICHER CULTURE
THAN THEIR BRAZEN CAPTORS DREAMED OF?

WHERE ARE THE GODS WHO TRUSTED STRANGERS
WORSHIPPING SYMBOLS MOCKING MEANING?
PILLAGED, PROSTRATE, BURNING, BLEEDING,
BURDENED BY THE CROSS THAT AWED THEM.

HERE IN THE BARRIO SEE THEIR SEED SIGH,
GROANING UNDER GRINGO BURDENS,
MOANING IN A FOREIGN JARGON,
WAITING FOR THE FINAL REFUGE.

SEE THE YOUNG MEN PITCHING COPPERS,
METAL THEIR FATHERS FORGED TO WEAPONS.
DESECRATED SEED WILL RIPEN
TO A FRUIT OF BURLESQUE SEMBLANCE.

SEE YOUNG WOMEN, STILL FULL BREASTED,
SPIRIT DEAD, BUT SUBSTANCE HAUNTED,
MINDS ENSLAVED BUT WOMBS UNDAUNTED,
BLED TO BREED NEW VALIANT SAVIORS.

NOW COMES AN AZTEC VIRGIN STALKING,
CALABASH BALANCED, REGAL POSTURE,
TO BATHE HER BASTARD IN AN OIL CAN,
PULQUE SPAWNED NEAR THE FECAL CORNER.

SLIM CHOICE WAITS THIS BAWLING SIBLING:
DRUDGE AND WANT, OR EKE BY THIEVING.
THESE THE PROSPECTS; HIS THE GRIEVING.
GRIM PAST PRESENTS FOR A FUTURE.

WHO WILL HELP THESE FECKLESS CHILDREN?
FATHERS, MOTHERS, HAPLESS, HOPELESS?
WHO WILL GRAFT INTO THE BARRIOS
PRIDE AND WISDOM, RUNNING WATER?

WHERE ARE THE WHITE HEIRS OF HIDALGO?
WHERE IS THE BREED OF FRAY MORELOS?
JUAREZ WAS THE LAST PURE STATESMAN
STRIVING FOR HIS STRUGGLING PEOPLE.

AVARICE HOVERS IN PALSIED POWER,
BLOATED ON FLESH, BLACK TROPIC BUZZARD,
FAT WITH THE SWEAT OF PEON VICTIMS,
THIS THE BARRIO'S SCREAMING EAGLE.

PERCHED ON THE CROSS OF ALMS COLLECTORS,
STAMPED IN THE BADGE OF TAX INSPECTORS,
PRESSED IN THE SEAL OF STRUMPET JUDGES,
NESTING IN BREASTS OF POLITICIANS.

SWINK IN THE BARRIO, SONS OF TLALPAN.
DREAM NOT OF DAYS OF ANTIQUE GRANDEUR.
DREAM NOW OF BUZZARD-SCOURGING HEROES.
WAIT THEIR ADVENT, PITCHING COPPERS.

VIETNAM VET IN A BOX

BEATEN DOWN BY UNRECORDED BURDENS
HUDDLED IN THE RANCID STAIRWELL CORNER
HE LIES ENCOFFINED IN CASTOFF CARDBOARD
VENTED BY THE SWIRLING CHILL
OF TUNNELED GUSTS
SHRIEKING OF RATTLING TRAINS.

DEFYING SHUDDERS OF SNOW
SWIRLING DOWN STEELLIPPED STEPS
HE SLEEPS, OR IS HE DEAD
IN HIS WELTER OF CAMOUFLAGE RAGS?

SCHEDULED HEELS CLICK BY
HASTENING TO AGENDAS
LANCING HURRIED GLANCES
AT THE BUNDLED CLUTTER
HARRIED BY INDIFFERENT GUILT
SHIVERING AT THE PROSPECT
OF A CITY'S COLD TRAVAIL
BEYOND THE GAPING DOORWAY
INFINITY'S PITILESS SKY.

ON THE SUBTLETIES OF DEARTH

HUNGER IS A SILENT VILLAIN
STEALTHY, STEADFAST, PATIENT, SLY,
NIBBLING AT THE MIND AND SPIRIT,
MUNCHING MUMLY, DAY BY DAY.

BRAZEN EVILS EARN MORE FANFARE;
WANT IS EVER UNDERPAID,
HUMBLE MUMMER, GREY MASKED CHORUS,
MUTED IN A MASK OF PRIDE.

IF THE MASK BE BURST BY YEARNING,
SENSE AND FEELING FUSE, BERSERK,
NEED IN NAKED, CANDID HORROR
STALKS FROM SQUALOR, SCRAWN AND STARK.

IF LOVE'S LACK STRETCH TAUT THE SPIRIT,
STOMACH SATED, HEART DENIED,
GLUT AND GAUD PROVE GRIMLY FUTILE,
PLENTY IS A BLEAK FACADE.

SECURITY

A CHILD OF WANT,
I ACCUMULATE.
BUT NEVER QUITE THE MEASURE
TO ASSUAGE A FEAR OF NEED.
HOW MUCH CAN BE ENOUGH?

KURDISTAN, SARAJEVO, PORT AU PRINCE, ETC.

HORDES OF HUNGER FREEZE ATOP HIGH PASSES,
FIELDS OF NEED STRETCH WRETCHED
PAST HORIZONS.
GIRDLES OF HATRED STARVE
BLEAK WATERLESS CITIES
WHERE WOMEN WEEP IN RAVAGED DESPAIR,
AND CHILDREN WHIMPER, STARVING.
DRUG-GORGED GOONS
AND MINDLESS MUSCLED VENGEANCE
PLAY WITH IMPUNITY TYRANNY'S ANCIENT GAMES.
BARE FEET ON ICY ROCK BLEED TRAILS OF TREASON
BY SLEEK EFFETES REASONING IN SHRUGS.
WHILE IDLE KNIGHTS MASSED IN MOTTLED BEIGE
WATCH GLUMLY, SHAMED AND SILENT,
ARMS AT REST BEHIND TIMIDITY'S BARRIERS,
IMMOBILIZED BY FACELESS NAMELESS MEN
DEBATING IN SUMPTUOUS LUNCH
WHILE REMNANT LEGIONS OF THE DAMNED
LOOSE HAVOC UNRESTRAINED
UPON THE HELPLESS HOPELESS.

CAIDOS

ZARAGOZA

BEAT THE PRIESTS AGAIN
GOD WILL BROOK NO REBELS
TRUSS THE STUDENTS TIGHT
FAITH WILL NOT ENDURE
STRIKES
ASSURE TAUT CONTROL

IF BISHOPS LOSE THEIR PAWNS
A SANCTITY OF CENTURIES WILL BREAK
THE FLINTIEST SPIRIT
SOFTENS IN OUR VICE

ONE VOICE IS HEARD
INTONED
INCARNATE WORD
WE WORSHIP THEE
ABJECT HUMILITY
BECOMES THE AGENTS OF GOD

GRACE IN WORLDLINESS
ERODED SPIRIT IN THE PAST
UNHINGED EXCESS
CORRUPTED UNHALLOWED NATIONS
GAIN GLORY WITH SUCCESS
BEAT THE PRIESTS AGAIN

DUMPING EXCESS BAGGAGE

WITHIN THE PROFESSION,
AND JUST BETWEEN COLLEAGUES,
THIS ALIEN WENCH CAME ACROSS THE BORDER
AT MIDNIGHT
IN A TAXI, NO LESS,
TO DELIVER A YANKEE CHILD.
SHE ARRIVED DISTENDED FIVE CENTIMETERS.
MARGINAL, YOU'LL AGREE,
BUT STILL ENOUGH TIME FOR QUICK ACTION.
I'D HAD THIS HEAVY DAY.
WITH MY NEW SLURPER
I CAN EASILY DO THREE DOZEN ABORTS PER DIEM,
WITH TIGHT SCHEDULING, EVEN MORE.
FIGURE IT OUT, AT FIVE HUNDRED PER.
AND THERE ARE THOSE OTHER BENEFITS...
SOME OF THEM ARE REALLY DEPRAVED
DEPRIVED, AND OHSOGRATEFUL.
ANYWAY, I WAS BUSHED,
AND BUSY WITH AN OVERDUE DELIVERY,
SO WE CALLED ANOTHER CAB
AND SENT HER ON TO COUNTY.
THEY HAVE A TOLERABLE OB-GYN
ONLY TWELVE MILES AWAY.
I'M ALMOST SURE SHE MADE IT OK,
AND WE HAVE ANOTHER CITIZEN
TO BE WEANED WITHIN OUR BORDERS,
TO CLOTHE AND FEED
AND GIVE FREE MEDICAL SERVICE.

FITTING IN EDUCATION

WITH CAPTIVATING SMILES, BEGUILING EYES,
BUBBLING EFFERVESCENCE
MISS BUSHNELL LED US
TO A THICKET OF GOOD FEELINGS,
TOGETHERNESS,
INTEGRATED SOCIAL HARMONY.
SPORTS LETTERS WERE HER SPECIAL PRIDE
LEADERSHIP AND CHEERING FOR THE GIRLS.
WE SUBTLY UNDERSTOOD
THE INUTILITY, THE SOCIAL COSTS OF STUDY
OF LEARNING UNPROFITABLE FACTS
IRRELEVANT DATES
MATH BEYOND THE LEDGER LEVEL,
ALIEN LANGUAGES ONE WOULD NEVER USE
FRUITLESS FRUITS OF A FORGOTTEN PAST.
EXCEPT FOR RALPH, THE QUIET MISFIT.
BOOKBURDENED, QUICKEYED, DRABCLOTHED,
RELUCTANT TO JOIN IN SOCIALIZING GAMES
UNWILLING TO STRIVE FOR CAMPUS FAME
UNABLE TO FIT THE GLOSSY MOLD
HE UTTERED LITTLE
AND THEN, OF BORING THINGS
LIKE PTERODACTYL WINGS,
PENTAMETER,
AND DINGY KINGS SO DEADLY DULL.
RALPH WROTE OUT STRINGS OF KNOTTED DATES

OF NOTABLE NAMES
BRANCHED PARAGRAPHS
OF ACCUMULATED THOUGHT

PEDESTALS OF THE PRESENT, HE CONFIDED
WHEN JENNIFER, CURIOUS AND COY,
CHARMED HIM FOR A LARK ONE DRIZZLY DAY.
TO RALPH THE GREEKS WERE NOT A COLLEGE GOAL
BUT LIVING DEAD COMPANIONS HE DEBATED.
POOR RALPH, WE TISKED THAT HE WAS EVER BORN
A TOLERATED BUTT OF SMIRKING SCORN.

AT OUR TWENTY-FIFTH REUNION
IN THE MIDST OF GIGGLES AND SCREAMS
JABS, JIBES, ATTENUATED DREAMS,
CONVOYED GOALS SECURE IN PLACID SEAS,
MISS BUSHNELL, A HUB OF GREYING CHARM
ASSEMBLED COURT, HUGGING EVERY MINION
REHEARSING WITH UNFEIGNED EXCITATATION
LISTLESS LISTS OF AFFABLE NETWORKS
LIMITED GOALS AND MODERATE ACHIEVEMENTS.

I REMEMBERED FOR A WINK IN THE ECHOES OF TIME
AN EARLY VISION, TARNISHED AND ENTOMBED
OF SINGING RIGGING SURGING HIGH
ABOVE ABYSSAL DEPTHS OF ASPIRATION
THE SOLITARY RISK OF STRETCHED ACHIEVEMENT
AND DREAMED AGAIN OF A NOBLE COMPANY
UNKNOWN BUT KNOWABLE

GATHERED BY THE GODS
ON THE GASPING SURGE OF CRESTS,
IN THE DIZZYING SUCK OF TROUGHS,
HIGH AND LOW TOGETHER
INTENSE, ENGAGED, ENTHRALLED,
NAVIGATING THE FUTURE
APPALLED BY SHALLOW WATER.

A SHOUT, AMIDST THE CELEBRATION.
RALPH'S NAME WAS THROWN OUT,
BUT HE WAS FOUND NOT PRESENT.
THERE WAS A RUMOR, JENNIFER REPORTED
OF SOME VAGUE OCCUPATION,
REMOTE AND GRUBBING
HAVING TO DO WITH NERDLY TRIVIA,
COMPLICATED MATH, ASTROPHYSICS, STARS, …
THAT KIND OF THING.
MISS BUSHNELL SMILED CHARITABLY
AND SIGHED
RALPH NEVER DID FIT IN.

WINNERS

WE RUN THE DEMON COURSE
WITH SPRINTER'S SPEED
HEADS BOWED, EYES FOCUSSED FORE SWIFT FEET
IMPELLED BY GREED.
NO GOAL, NO CHART,
NO SIDE OR BACKWARD GLIMPSE,
NOR PAUSE FOR HEED NOR HELP
FOR ONE WHO LIMPS.
WE HASTEN ON!

ASK NOT TO SEE THE ORDINANCES WE BEAR.
SEARCH NOT OUR ULTIMATE ABODE;
IT IS NOWHERE.
NOR QUERY US FOR REASON OF OUR HASTE,
NOR PREACH TO US OF WANTONNESS AND WASTE.
WE HASTEN ON!

AND WHEN OUR SINEWS FAIL US IN THE RACE
LET OUR SOLE EULOGY BY THIS:
THEY KEPT THE PACE
AMID THE RAGING TORRENT OF THE STRONG.
BUT NOW THE PATH IMPELS, THE COURSE IS LONG.
WE HASTEN ON!

INCIDENTALS

A BABBLE OF TRIBES

A BABBLE OF TRIBES DIVIDES US,
EACH ASSERTING THE ONLY TRUE,
INSISTING ITS VIRTUES EXCLUSIVE, UNIQUE,
SHOUTING TO DROWN DRY DOUBT,
RULING OUT OTHERS' UBIQUITOUS NEEDS, VALUES, GOALS,
COMMON REACTIONS AND DEEDS
WHEN RECURRING CONDITIONS OCCUR.
CAN'T WE DEVELOP ONE LANGUAGE, ONE ETHIC
COMMON ATOP THE TRIBES?
ENGLISH, SPANISH, RUSSIAN, CHINESE...
QUELLE DIFFERENCE?
PERHAPS A CIRCUS OF INTERLINGUAL CIRCUITS?
A THESAURUS OF COMMON THOUGHT
TRANSLATED BY SHOCK
OF MIRRORED RECOGNITION?
ONE TONGUE, ONE PULSE TO LICK MYOPIC FEAR
OF WE AGAINST ALL OTHERS,
OF THEIR INFERIOR VIEWS,
OF OUR SUPERIOR TRUTHS,
ENDOWMENTS FROM ON HIGH?
MUST WE REMAIN TOO PROUD TO HEED OR HEAR
SOFT OFT-REASONED MURMURS OF INFINITY,
CATASTROPHES BY PURBLIND TRIBES DOWN HERE?

ADMONITION

PROPER IS A POMPOUS WORD
SMUGLY SNIDE, LIKE LIE, ABSURD.
EXCESSIVE STYLE
UNTEMPERED, STRONG,
IS ALWAYS, ABSOLUTELY WRONG.

AFTER SCHOPENHAUER

I AM THE CENTER OF THE UNIVERSE,
NEEDING NO ONE'S PRAISE
HEEDING NO ONE'S CENSURE
SAVE MY OWN.
MY NOW IS THE HUB OF ALL BENT TIME,
INFORMED, ENHANCED, REFINED
BY WINNOWED MINDS
FROM CULTURES, AGES PRESENT, PAST,
AMALGAMATED HERE AT LAST
IN MY WILLFUL JUDGMENT,
RULED AND OVERULED INTUITIVELY
BY ULTIMATE FORCE
AND LAW OF COSMIC NATURE,
IMPRESSED, EXPRESSED IN MYSTIC FORMULATION
BY MICROMINUTE, UNLIMITED, UNFATHOMABLE BEING

AT THE OBELISK

ANCIENT WHEN OUR ANCIENT WAS UNDREAMED,
ERODED WHEN BRONZED LEGIONS MARCHED ON AN
TO DESECRATE THE SUN GOD'S HALLOWED SEE,
AND DECORATE THEIR PROFANE GREEK GODS' CITY
WITH PHALLIC TROPHIES OF A SUBJECT CREED,
THIS CRABBED STONE,
SUCKED TO THE NEWEST VORTEX
OF PROGRESS AND POWER,
HAS SPITTED SUCCESSIVE SUCCESSES LIKE THE SUN
THROUGHOUT EVOLVING TIME,
GNOMEN SUPERLATIVE,
POINTING EVER FROM THE PINNACLES OF POMP.

DEATH IS A SWIVELHIPPED HARLOT
LIFE IS A WITHERLIPPED MONK

AROUND THIS SHADOWLESS BASE
EVEN THE UTMOST GREEKS ONCE PROBED FOR LIGHT
CHRIST WAS HID,
NAPOLEON PARADED,
AND INSIGNIFICANCES HAVE LOITERED
THROUGHOUT IMPROVING AGES
TO PICK AT DEADLOCKS
OLD WHEN BETTER WAS NEW.

AROUND THIS PENSIVE PEN
TERRACED CONFORMITIES OF INTERLOCKING ORDER
BRIGHT AND HARD IN EARLY SPRING'S ICED SKY,
MASTERS OVER SEASONS,
FROWN DOWN UPON THE UNENLIGHTENED PATCH.

STARK RINGING TREES
WHISPER COMPELLING REASONS
FOR SCENTED PASTELS
TO GARLAND THE FADED RED RELIC.
COLD LIMBS BLOW OUT SOFT, NUDGING BUDS,
DULL, PRISTINE PROMISE
TO BUDGE BLEAK, BARREN BLACKNESS
FROM EACH BRANCH.
BROWN FURZE
GREENING A VELVET GRAIN
PERCEPTIBLE TO IMPERFECTED CREATURES
BEGUILES EYE LISTENING SQUIRRELS,
GAY, GREY TAILORED, SCYTHE TAILED,
TO RIPPLE AND FLIT
GIDDY
ON A FRAGRANCE NEVER UTTERED,
SENSED, NOT SAID.

LIFE IS A SWIVELHIPPED HARLOT
DEATH IS A WITHERLIPPED MONK

HOW FAR HAVE WE COME
SINCE THUTMOS MARCHED ON TYRE?
GROSS, IMMEMORIAL PASSIONS PRESS US CLOSE
DESPITE MIRACULOUS STEPS.
GREED STILL DRIVES HIS CHARIOT;
SIX KINDRED, AGELESS CHURLS CAVORT UNBRIDLED.
MEANING, TUFTED AND LACED
WITH CONGERIES OF THINGS,
ANNOTATED, FORMULATED, COORDINATED
REMAINS A SHADOWED TAPESTRY,
WARP OF PARADOX,
WOOF OF MYSTERY,
REALITY UNDEFINED.

RIOT, CONNIVE, THRIVE DIE
FAST, FEEL, AND LIVE

CONTRACT IS THE HIGHEST LAW
IN THE REALM OF MINE AND THINE.
RIGHT IS MISTAKEN FOR EQUITY,
TITLE EQUATED WITH DEED.
ETHICS REMAINS A CODE
FOR APPORTIONING THINGS.
THE SPIGOT OF ABUNDANCE
TRICKLES
HELD FAST BY PRINCIPLED HANDS
WITH INTERESTS CONSTRUED TOO COMMON.
MEN CONFORM TO MATTER.

IS IT IN MAN'S INTEREST
TO PROFIT FROM MAN?
THIS IS THE SIN OF COMMISSION:
THAT PSEUDO REALISTS
KNOWING THE MARKET OF EVERY GOOD,
THE HUMAN VALUE OF NONE,
IMPOSE THEIR INNER QUALMS
AS VAGUE AS PAIN REMEMBERED,
AS HAUNTING AS ITS DREAD,
UPON BELIEVING MINIONS.
LEADERS KNEAD THE CREDULOUS
TO CURSE FATE'S PRESS
ENTHRALLED WITH VAINGLORIOUS VISIONS
NUMB WITH THE WINE OF REGRET.

RIOT, CONNIVE, THRIVE, LIVE
FAST, FEEL, AND DIE

WE WHO HAVE RECKONED
THE TIMELESSNESS OF TIME,
SUBDIVIDED INFINITY,
AND UNDERTAKEN
INSTALLATION OF IMPROVEMENTS
THROUGHOUT GOD'S EMINENT DOMAIN,
STILL HOMESTEAD ON THE BORDERLANDS OF SELF,
DELUDED THAT GETTING IS GAIN,
THAT GIVING IS LOSS.
THE FLACCID HAND OF GREED
POSTS IRONY'S LEDGER.

DEATH IS A SWIVELHIPPED HARLOT
LIFE IS A WITHERLIPPED MONK
RIOT, CONNIVE, THRIVE, DIE
FAST, FEEL, AND LIVE

WE LIVE IN ERROR STILL,
AND DIE IN DOUBT
FAILING THE ETERNAL TEST
RECONCILIATION
OF BELLY TO BRAIN.

COUNSEL

ALL HUMAN SPEECH IS JUST SELF-JUSTIFICATION
SOOTHING, SCORNING, HELPFUL, WISTFUL, WISE,
IT BUT SUPPORTS THE SPEAKER'S EQUILIBRIUM,
RATIONALIZING A PRECARIOUS BALANCE
ON THE EDGE OF TIME,
A MODEL FOR THE MUDDLED
GUIDING GLIB TOWARD MURKY DESTINATIONS,
AT BEST IMPELLED
BY UNACKNOWLEDGED MENTORS,
UNCONFRONTED DEMONS,
AT WORST BY TREASON FOR MONEY.
THE BEST ADVICE IS SILENCE, EARSHUT THOUGHT
COERCION OF THE UNTONED MIND TO REASON.

CRITERIA

THINGS ARE MEASURED BY METAL
    AND PAPER OF SHIFTING VALUE
NO BOOKS ARE KEPT
    ON VITAL ACCOUNTS OF WORTH.

FADING GRATITUDE, RIBBONS, CERTIFICATES
SETTLE OUR VITAL DEBTS:
    LOVE, PATIENCE, HONOR, SACRIFICE...
THE KNOWINGS AND THE GNAWINGS
    OF THE HEART
THAT MAKE LIFE WORTH A STRIVING.

WILL METAL FANCIERS, PAPER COUNTERS,
                TOY COLLECTORS
EVER GLIMPSE THE VISION?

DAD

WHEN 1 WAS CALLOW
AND HEADY WITH SAP,
FATHER WAS A FIGURE OF VAGUE SHAME
WHO NEVER FOUGHT
AND YET PREVAILED
BY SMILING
INEXPLICABLY
ENGULFING MY UNCOMPASSED DRIVES
IN SILENT, PLODDING PATIENCE.

DREAMSCAPE

EACH MAN PLAYS TO HIMSELF THE HERO'S PART,
IMAGINES ALL HIS ACTIONS THINGS APART
FROM DULL AND FRUITLESS, NIGGARD,
COMMON DEEDS,
ENVISIONS THAT HE SATES HIS DAILY NEEDS
IMPENDING GREATER GLORIES SOON TO COME.
AND THOUGH THE YEARS PLOD BY,
THEIR MOUNTING SUM
AMASSING MEAGER CREDITS TO HIS NAME,
ENTICING, SELDOM CROWNING HIM WITH FAME,
THE WISTFUL DREAMER TOILS ON, BLIND WITH HOPE,
RELYING ON A FATE BEYOND HIS SCOPE
TO FAVOR HIM AT LAST WITH VAST SUCCESS,
AWARDING HIM THE HERO'S GRAND LARGESSE.
EACH ACTOR MIMES HIS MUDDLED ROLE
WITH YEARNING HEART,
MOCKED FROM BREATH TO BREATH
BY ILLUSIONS OF HIS PART.

ENTOMBED IN THE STACKS

WHILE PURBLIND BILLIONS STRIVE TO SURVIVE
IN FRENETIC CAMPAIGNS ON THE RIM,
I HAVE COMPASSED MYSELF—
AN INTERLOPER AMONG INDIFFERENT FRIENDS—
HERE IN THE COOL, CALM
DIM RETREAT OF THE SELECT
INTELLECTS FROM AGES PAST,
CONSTANT TO ETERNITY,
VOICES ETCHED IN PAPER STONE
MARKING THE TESTED WAYS
TO SURVEY WHERE WE ARE,
WHERE WE HAVE BEEN,
WHERE WE PERHAPS MAY GO,
SHOULD GO,
WOULD GO
IF NONPAROCHIAL WISDOM WERE TO PREVAIL
WARY WITH WISDOM
        OF BOTTOMLESS HATEFUL TRAPS,
SECURE IN POSITIVE VISTAS
WITH ETHICS OF ABUNDANCE
TO BURY HUNGER, BROTHERIZE TRIBES,
        PRECLUDE INFIRMITY, DISEASE,
SHRINK SPACE, FUSE RACE TO RACE,
RAISE SIGHTINGS
FROM BRUTE SURVIVAL
TO NOBLE GRACE.

REVIEWING THESE ANNALS ENTAILS
PENSIVE SEARCHING ALONG A MAZE OF TRAILS
BEATEN, FORGOTTEN, RENEWED
RICH WITH CAPTIVATING TANGLES
IN THE HARRIED JUNGLE OF TIME.
THE TASK:
TO STRING FAR FOUND JEWELS OF THOUGHT
INTO COHERENT CLUSTERS
IN A DIADEM OF COMPREHENSIVE TRUTH,
ALL MEAN, MYOPIC ARGUMENTS QUASHED,
NOTHING SIGNIFICANT LOST,
NOTHING SUPERFLUOUS ADDED,
ALL ENCOMPASSED AND INTERTWINED
IN RIGOROUS DAZZLING BEAUTY.

EVENING

ABOVE THE ROOFTOPS WISPS OF SAFFRON CLOUD
BLAZE RAW AGAINST THE TWILIGHT'S
FRAGILE MAUVE.
A PINPOINT PLANET GLISTENS
THROUGH THE SHROUD
OF SPECTRAL SHADE NEW RISING IN THE COVE
OF WANING LIGHT THAT LAGS BEHIND THE SUN,
LOATH TO CONCEDE THE ATMOSPHERE TO DUSK.
THE FIERCE CLOUDFIRES WANE. EMBERS OF DUN
SUPPLANT THE FLAMES, DULL REMNANTS,
TINTS OF MUSK
AMID THE BLUEBLACK FRAGRANCE OF THE NIGHT.
NOCTURNAL OVERTONES PERVADE THE SKY.
THE PLANET BURNS IN CONTRAST YET MORE BRIGHT
AS COOLING SOLAR WAVES NOW SOFTLY HIE
BEYOND THE RIM TO NURTURE NEIGHBOR REALMS,
A BOLD
BLITHE HARBINGER
OF MIDNIGHT'S STAR ENCRUSTED MOLD.

11.65

BARREN TREES, PALE SKY
BLACK BRITTLE FINGERS, REACHING.
HOPE WAITS PATIENTLY.

11.90

FLAMING HUES ERUPT IN LEAVES,
OLD LIMBS DRAIN GREEN VIGOR.
CALM DEATH IS BEAUTY.

MVP EMERITUS

IN THE ROUND WORLD'S SHADOWED CORNERS
YESTERDAY'S HERO SITS SLACK
RECALLING ENCORES AND ECHOES
DREAMING IN TIME ROLLED BACK.

MEM'RIES OF FRENZIED OVATIONS
RUSHES FROM TESTING STRONG FLESH
THE HUSH OF THE CRITICAL MOMENT
THE CRUSH OF STEEL-MUSCLED SUCCESS

SKINBURSTING ELATION OF WINNING
GONE SOFT IN THE FLAB OF TIME
SERENE, THE AGING CONTENDER
SMILES INWARDLY, WISTFUL, SUBLIME.

1.93

FRAGILE BLOSSOMS
CRACKED BLACK LIMBS
THE FULL MOON BLOOMS IN PERFUMED NIGHT.

PROGRESS REPORT

FOUR HUNDRED OF THE ENEMY WERE SLAIN
THIS AFTERNOON.
AT LEAST ONE THOUSAND MAIMED
WERE CARRIED OFF.
HISTORIC RATIOS SUGGEST
SURVIVORS WILL INCLUDE:
SIX TWENTY TWO POINT NINER CRIPPLED
BY METALLIC FRAGMENTS;
THREE TWENTY FIVE POINT FOUR
SEVERELY BURNED
(POSE NO FURTHER MENACE);
THIRTY THREE POINT ONE
ONLY MODERATELY BURNED,
BUT PHYSICALLY IMPAIRED;
SEVENTY SIX POINT SEVENTEEN
CHEMICALLY RETIRED.
THE REMAINDER ARE CLASSIFIED IN
INSIGNIFICANT FIGURES.
NO AGE/SEX BREAKDOWNS
HAVE BEEN RELEASED.

UNCONFIRMED RUMORS OF CIVILIAN DEATHS
DUE TO RELEASE OF JELLIED GASOLINE
ON HOMES INSTEAD OF FACTORIES ADJOINING
ARE RELIABLY REPORTED
TO BE EXAGGERATIONS.
"THE ACTS OF WAR,

A SPOKESMAN CLARIFIED,
ARE STILL AN ART,
AN INEXACT PROFESSION.
MISTAKES OCCUR,
DESPITE OUR BEST INTENTION."

THE EXTREMIST FOREIGN PRESS
HAS STILL ADDUCED NO PROOF
SUPPORTING RECENT SLANDEROUS ALLEGATIONS
THAT THE PRESIDENTIAL ASSASSINATION
WAS OUR COUNTER-INTELLIGENCE ACTION.

REPRESENTATIVES OF THE RESPONSIBLE MEDIA
HAVE WELCOMED MARTIAL LAW,
TO GUARD THEIR MOVEMENTS
SCREEN OUT PROPAGANDA
HARMFUL TO OUR CAUSE,
DANGEROUS TO PUBLIC MORALS,
AND DISRUPTIVE TO INTERNAL ORDER.

THE ANTI-CORRUPTION CORPS
CONTINUED INCESSANT WAR
ON BLACK MARKETEERING LAST NIGHT
WITH A FLASH MIDNIGHT RAID
ON SHOPS COVERTLY STOCKED
WITH GOODS SUGGESTING
ILLICIT POSSESSION.
TWO WOMEN CLERKS WERE PLACED
IN GOVERNMENT PRISON.

THE COMMANDING OFFICER OF MILITARY STORES
HAS BEEN SEVERELY LECTURED
FOR STOCK SHORTAGES FOUND
AT SEVERAL INSTALLATIONS.

ADDITIONAL RUMORS OF TORTURE
OF PEASANT YOUTHS SAID TO HAVE DIED
WHILE UNDER INTERROGATION
HAVE PROMPTED AN UNNAMED SOURCE
IN THE GOVERNMENT
OF OUR GENEROUS ALLY
TO CLARIFY THE PRISONER SITUATION:

"AS GUESTS OF A SOVEREIGN NATION,
IT WOULD NOT HAVE CEMENTED RELATIONS
FOR OUR ADVISORS PRESENT AT THESE DEATHS
TO INTERFERE WITH LOCAL JURISDICTION.
THIS IS A PRINCIPAL OF FREEDOM,
ACCLAIMED BY EVERY NATION
OF THE PEOPLE, BY THE PEOPLE,
AND FOR THE PEOPLE."

AND NOW, OUR NATIONAL ANTHEM...

RECONSIDERATIONS

NOW, HOSTING THEIR STUDENT GRANDSONS,
BUYING THEIR GOODS, BORROWING THEIR MONEY,
SEEING THEM PREVAIL
IN THE VERY REALMS WE FOUGHT THROUGH FLAME TO RULE,
I WONDER WHAT THE FIGHTING WAS ABOUT,
THEY SEEM AS CIVILIZED AS WE—PERHAPS MORESO,
A COURTEOUS CULTURE, WITH HONOR STILL INTACT.
ATROCITIES THERE WERE,
BUT WE COMMITTED A SHARE
NEVER ADMITTED, NEVER REPORTED,
BUT WITNESSED AT THE FRONTS.
WAS IT ALL ONLY TO SETTLE WHICH CLIQUES—
UNNAMED, UNSEEN, UNKNOWN—
WOULD SEIZE OR KEEP THE POWER?
WAS MANHOOD EARNED BY MILLIONS
WITH DEATH THEIR DAILY PAY
SO BANKERS DUM, NOT BANKERS DEE,
CAN NOW COMMAND OUR INTEREST?
IS SPOILS CONTROL THE STAFF OF EVERY FLAG?
WAS IT ALL FOR DIVIDENDS AND DOLLARS?
IS VALOR OUR ONLY LONG TERM GAIN FROM WAR?

REFLECTIONS IN A PERJURED GLASS

WHAT I AM
I ALWAYS WAS
AND STILL AM MORE BECOMING
ALWAYS BECOMING,
I NEVER AM
UNLESS I AM
BECOMING.

SEATTLE VISTA

WHEN I BEHOLD A CITY VAST AND CALM
BENEATH THE DEEPENING SHADES OF TWILIGHT SKY
A PEACE PERVADES MY SPIRIT, LIKE A BALM
APPLIED BY LOVING HANDS, MOST SOOTHINGLY
UPON THE THROBBING SORES OF NOONDAY STRIFE.
THE NIGHT AIR FILTERED DRONE OF UMBRAL ZEST,
THE DRAWLING, CRAWLING,
BURGEONING EVENING LIFE
ARISING FROM ITS TORPID VESPER REST
REKINDLES WITH ITS NASCENT RISING SURGE
MY WANING STRENGTH TO SENSE, MY APPITITE
TO FEEL ALL LIFE, MY SOUL'S PRIMORDIAL URGE
TO SOAR INTO THE CLEAR, UNFATHOMED NIGHT
AND WITH A WRAITHLIKE, UNIMPASSIONED
MYRIAD EYE
TO PONDER MAN, AND FIND AN ANSWER TO MY WHY.

SENSIBLE CALCULATIONS

IS THERE A RANGE OF FEELINGS
WHICH CAN BE TYPED AND MEASURED?
ARE LOVE AND NEED, FEAR AND GREED
REFINABLE TO NUMBERS,
REDUCING THE MYSTIC MASS
OF EMOTION COMMUNION
TO WEIGHTED HUMAN FACTORS?

CAN A THREE-FOUR-FIVE OF SENSES
BECOME COORDINATE LOGIC,
GEODESICS OF SELF,
MEASURED INTERVALS OF CHAOTIC ACTION,
GLANDULAR DIMENSIONS,
PRIMARY, SECONDARY EQUATIONS
OF HOPE AND DESPAIR?

CAN THE QUINTESSENTIAL PROTON
NOW'S FRENETIC PASSION
BECOME KINETIC REASON,
A STEADY STATE,
POTENTIAL CALCULATED,
SPACETIMED,
THOUGHTFELT?

SHIMMERING AVENUE

IN MY BOAT AT NIGHT AT SEA
A MOONBEAM ROADWAY FOLLOWS ME.
WHERE 'ERE I DRIFT ATOP THE BLUE,
WHEN I LOOK UP, IT LEADS THERE, TOO.
IT BECKONS ME TO SAIL AFAR
DOWN SHIMMERING PATH TO THE LUNAR STAR
HUNG LOW AND FULL O'ER MISTY HILL,
SO SOFT AND WAN IT MAKES A CHILL
OF SECRET, SILENT ECSTACY
RUN DOWN MY SPINE. IT PLEASES ME
TO ALWAYS SEE THAT AVENUE
DRIFT STRAIGHT TO ME ACROSS THE BLUE.

10.90

BEIGE CONES DANGLE IN GREEN BOUGHS
SPLAYED AGAINST BLUE SKY.
HOW FUTILE IS AMBITION.

THE HIGHEST BANNER

HONOR FLIES ABOVE ALL FLAGS.
FAITHFUL CONSCIENCE BINDS THE BRAVE
TO HIGHER RULES BEYOND THE GRAVE.

HONOR STIFLES SQUINTING GREED,
SHAMES TO DUST THE BLACKHEART DEED,
CONVERTS BRASH LUST TO A HIGHER NEED.

HONOR SOARS ABOVE ALL STATES.
RACES, CREEDS BECOME SOULMATES.
ZEALOTS SKULK BEYOND ITS GATES.

GENTLE HONOR, PATIENT, STRONG,
ENDURES WITH VIGOR, STIFLING WRONG,
REJECTING DEEDS THAT DON'T BELONG.

HONOR LIVES; DISHONOR DIES.
TRUTH BESMIRCHED WITH OFFAL LIES
MAY SEEM TO FALL, BUT STILL WILL RISE.

WADING IN

TARAWA—NOVEMBER 20, 1943

THAT DAY WE WERE TO PLANT OUR FLAG
OVER THAT TROPICAL SPIT,
TO SQUEEZE OUR BOATS OVER THAT JAGGED REEF,
AND STORM ASHORE TO CONQUER
IN THUNDERING RAGE.

NAVY PLANNERS HOPED THERE WOULD BE
SUFFICIENT SEA
TO FLOAT OUR BOATS OVER THE REEF
TO THRUMBLE ACROSS THE PLACID BLUE LAGOON
FRONTING ENEMY GUNS
AND CONQUER WHAT WAS ONCE IDYLLIC SPLENDOR.
A MEAGER TIDE BETRAYED THE BRASSY GUESSWORK
GRISLY FORTUNE TRICKED THEM;
WE PICKED UP THE TAB.

"THIS IS AS FAR AS I GO!" OUR COXSWAIN CRIED
AS HE GROUNDED HIS CRAFT ON THE REEF,
DROPPING OUR ARMORED RAMP
IN THE FACE OF ZEROED GUNS
FIVE HUNDRED YARDS THIS SIDE
OF THE SANDY SHORE.

SILENT CURSING RIFLEMEN CHARGED FORWARD
INTO THE SEA.
THE HEAVIEST LADEN SANK, NO MORE TO RISE.
SURVIVORS, HELMETS TORTOISE LIKE,
TOILED TORTURED TOWARD THE SHORE
RIFLES HIGH OVER EACH HEAD
STRAINING, CURSING, PRAYING,
AGONIZED MUSCLES SLOW DANCING
THROUGH CHINHIGH TIDE,
THROUGH SWIRLS OF RED
HELPLESS TO DODGE FIERCE TORRENTS OF LEAD
HELLPELTING THE BLUE LAGOON.

AT LAST A REMNANT SURVIVING
STAGGERED UP THE SAND,
LUNGED FORWARD OVER THE SEAWALL
AND CHARGED BRUTE FATE
TO SETTLE OUR ACCOUNTS.

THREE DAYS LATER THE ISLAND FINALLY FELL,
ENEMY WIPED OUT IN DEFIANT DEFENSE
MOST OF OUR UNIT BOBBING NEAR THE SHORE
FLOATING BLOATED, BATTLE DRESSED,
A THANKSGIVING GIFT OF THE RISING TIDE.

WALKING WOUNDED—NAM

I AM NOT IMPRESSED BY THE RATIOS.
TWELVE-POINT-SIX OF LAST WEEK'S ENEMY DEAD
BALANCED ON THE COFFIN OF MY SON
IS NOT A SATISFYING FIGURE.
THERE IS NO COMPENSATION
IN MULTIPLES OF CARNAGE.
WHAT A PROFITLESS TOLL FOR EVERY MOTHER.
WHEN WILL THEY RECKON US
IN WOUNDS NOT MORTAL?
VAINGLORIOUS MEN WHO BOAST SUCH NEWS
MERELY MIGHT AMUSE BEFORE REVOLTING US
IF THEY WERE BRUTISH BOYS,
BUT SEMBLED SAFE IN POWER
FAR FROM THE BATTLE LINES
WHAT CAN THEY ACHIEVE?
DOMINION IN A WORLD NOT BETTER RULED?
THERE IS A GENERAL SICKNESS IN TOO MANY LANDS.
TOO MANY TRADERS PEDDLE TERRIBLE TRASH
TO TOO MANY TRAITORS TO MAN.
BRASSY PARASITES BLEED
TOO MANY PEOPLES NUMBED BY NEED.

TOO MANY DRUMHEAD COURTS
SUPPRESS COMPASSIONATE CREEDS.
WHAT ARE SUCH MEN PROFITED?
COULD THEY BE AS VIRILE WITHOUT RIBBONS?
LIVE AS WELL CREATING AS BY KILLING?
WHY DO MEN HONOR THESE CABALS
OF RUTHLESS BLOODLETTERS?
HAS MY SON DIED TO PERPETUATE THEM?
WHAT BLESSING IS THERE TO US
WHEN SUCH MEN PREY?

WASTED EFFORT?

ASSAILED BY DOUBTS AND FEARS
CONSTRAINED BY UNWEPT TEARS
TO PRATE LAMENT FOR VICTIMS MUTE AND DEAD,
THE BARD INVERTEBRATE
RECOUNTS UPON HIS SLATE
THE SURFEIT FARE OF TRAGIC SIGHTS HE'S FED.

HIS TALENT ALL UNSURE
HIS AUDIENCE A BOOR
WHO NODS AND CLUCKS,
BUT YET DECLINES TO ACT,
HE SCORNS WITH CYNIC'S SNEER
EACH HYPOCRITE'S FALSE TEAR.
SOCIETY CONDEMNS HIS LACK OF TACT.

NO BUILDER OF VAST WORKS,
HIS THEORY PRATTLING IRKS
THAT BREED WHICH DOES AND WASTES
WITH LAVISH HAND.
THE SOLITAIRE'S SOON DEAD,
UNSURE THAT WHAT HE'S SAID
WAS JUST AND TRUE, OR BUT A FOOL'S DEMAND.

SUBMISSIONS

OVER THE HILL
FACING DOWN THE FINAL SLOPE
DISTANCE SHORT OR LONG IS ALL OBSCURE
    IN THE WAVERING HAZE OF CHANCE.
I PAUSE IN THE CABIN OF SOLACE,
SHUFFLING A SHEAF OF CRUMPLED EXPERIENCE
INDELIBLE GLIMPSES, INTENSITIES RECORDED,
STRUCTURED TO RELISH, CHERISH, COMPREHEND
PAIN, FEAR, DESPAIR, ENNUI, RAPTURE, JOY...
FRAGILE RECOLLECTIONS
    OF DISINTEGRATED TIME
PENNED AND DRAWERED WITH A SIGH
TO LIE IN TRUTH ABANDONED
    DOWN LONG TIME.
NOW, STILL VIVID FROM THE BLUR OF YEARS,
THIS AT LAST THEIR FIRST AND FINAL CHANCE
TO BE SEEN IN THE SUN BEFORE IT SILENT SINKS.

www.ingramcontent.com/pod-product-compliance
Ingram Content Group UK Ltd.
Pitfield, Milton Keynes, MK11 3LW, UK
UKHW040017200726
13854UKWH00001B/250